What Children Want

ABOUT MYSELF

I was born in Zurich on 22 October 1964. I spent the first 20 years of my life in the Zurich lowlands. Then I moved to the city and later to beautiful Lake Zurich. Alongside professional challenges, I constantly tried to be a perfect mother, wife and housewife. But it was not possible to reconcile everything. Most of you will experience this at some point. Today I am not perfect, but authentic, honest and above all happy. Happy, among other things, because I now have the serenity not to want to be perfect any more. This has given me the space to look back on the last almost 25 years. With the experiences I have had as a mother on the one hand and as a woman on the other, I believe I have done many things right in my life. But as my children have grown from babies to young adults, I also see some things that I would do differently today.

Sabine Brandt

WHAT CHILDREN WANT

Bibliographical information of the Deutsche Nationalbibliothek [German National Library]. The German National Library lists this publication in the Deutsche Nationalbibliografie [German National Bibliography]; detailed bibliographical data may be accessed on the internet at http://dnb.dnb.de.

Cover graphics: Alditiya Rakasiwi/ kitahiirah5/ 2113838153/ Shutterstock.com

Proofreading, typesetting, cover design, production and publishing: BoD – Books on Demand, Norderstedt

ISBN 978-3-7562-6511-4

INHALT

Foreword.   7

The essence of being a parent.   11

It all comes back to you.   15

Setting an example and letting experience happen .   19

A small mental leap   28

Honesty.   30

Love and self-love   33

Time, perhaps the most important gift of all.   39

Being consistent, or battling for victory and defeat . .   45

Encouragement or expectation?   50

Competition between siblings   54

Letting them go   61

What if you can't go on?.   64

Afterword   66

Some thoughts of young adults   68

FOREWORD

I am the mother of two wonderful children, a daughter (23) and a son (20), who both still live with me. A good three years ago, my ex-husband – also the father of the children – and I separated. Fortunately, despite some difficulties, we have managed to find a way forward that works for all of us and today we have a very friendly and respectful relationship with each other (see my book Trennung mit Herz – von Akzeptanz bis Zukunft [Separation with Heart – from Acceptance to Zero hour], www.sabinebrandt.ch). We will always remain a family!

Then I am also an aunt to many nieces and nephews, some of whom are already parents themselves. So I am surrounded by young people in my family as well as in my job, and I am always interested in what makes 'children' of all ages tick. What they think and feel, what they laugh or cry about. And how young parents pass on their childhood experiences or try to break through patterns.

As a mother or father, you always want the best for your children. But there are many moments when self-doubt and insecurity follow you through the day. There may be extreme life situations, illnesses, deaths or separations and thus phases where you feel you cannot care enough for your children because your own problems absorb you.

But above all, you don't know what it actually means to become or to be a mother or father. Besides the responsibility you take on for a human being – emotionally you remain a parent for the rest of your life – you are confronted with feelings and situations you never knew before. You can be overflowing with love, happiness and gratitude, but you can also reach your physical and psychological limits. Parenthood, with all its ups and downs, is something you can only learn on the job.

The biggest personal change I experienced when I became a mother was my emotional permeability, which suddenly became a part of me. It made me vulnerable, and I had to come to terms with that. Suddenly you discover sides of yourself that completely overwhelm you, like a new part of you that you just have to accept and embrace.

Looking back, I would do a few things differently in bringing up my children. But I also know that I did what I thought was best. And when I look at them today, I know that I did at least get some things right.

I am absolutely against wrapping children in cotton wool. Without guidelines or rules, children feel overwhelmed and lost. But I cannot say yes to a rigid and draconian style of upbringing either. If rigid limits are set and the children don't understand why, these limits are likely to be violated. Likewise, it is impossible to bring up all the children in a family in exactly the same way. It is much more important to know exactly what you want to pass on to the children: what values, strengths and skills. It really is a major and very challenging task to have children and to bring them up. Nevertheless, parents should not let themselves be taken over by it completely. For this very reason, I am still convinced that it does no harm to the children if both parents work and they are partly looked after by others – always provided that things are well organised.

I have fond memories of my own childhood that make me feel exactly what I would like to pass on to my children in turn. When I left home, my older brothers and I were often invited to our parents' house for dinner on Sunday evenings. It was a homecoming full of warmth and security, even stronger than when we still lived there. Everything had been got ready, we were spoiled and their time belonged to us. Today, when I visit my 93-year-old mother, it is often still like that: that cosy, familiar feeling of being looked after. And that's exactly what I want to be able to put into practice with my children when we no longer live under the same roof: a warm and loving relationship, a joy in each other's company and an interested and honest togetherness.

But unfortunately, as we all know, the conditions are not always right for childhood to unfold in a loving and healthy home – this in an area where you are supposed to get the necessary soft skills for your future life.

So what do children really need? Besides a nice home, warm clothes and a few toys? Actually, they are simply things that everyone wants and that everyone can give, whether they are young or old. I call them 'things of the heart' – like affection, attention, love, security, honesty. The order does not matter here. In exchanges with my own children, my nieces and nephews and young adult friends, I have learned a lot that I would have liked to have known earlier. To ensure that these insights and experiences are not lost, I would like to pass them on to you and perhaps you can pass them on to your children. I hope that at the end of the book you will be glad you have read it. Not so much as a guidebook, but more as a report on the experiences of a mum who is very proud of her two children and therefore also a little bit proud of herself. Maybe, whatever your fears and doubts, you will sometimes recognise yourself in it too.

THE ESSENCE OF BEING A PARENT

Being a parent means living by new rules and being willing to invest a lot of time. If you can manage that, you will be rewarded with the most beautiful life experience ever.

Every couple who decide to become parents will try to master this task to the best of their knowledge and ability. But the know-how, and above all the feeling for being a parent can only be acquired on the job. Everything you read and hear about it can support you on your way, both individually and as a family, but it can also make you feel incredibly insecure. Every child, every adult and therefore every family is individual and unique, and so is the development of every single family member. No matter how well you prepare for your role, you don't know what becoming and being a parent will do to you. This can start with problems during pregnancy, hormones or sudden fears about the time to come and the responsibility. These are issues that can affect you emotionally in an unusual way as a future mother or father. There are feelings that have never been there before. For fathers, the fact that their partner feels more than 100 % mother in the beginning may not be easy to accept. From the start, your son or daughter rules the day and the night. They are dependent on you. However calm, stable and modern in your thinking you may be, the new situation can overwhelm you as a mother or father. Hopefully, the feeling of joy will outweigh this. But you get very little sleep and have to deal with your family first and foremost, you won't have so much time for your hobbies or for yourself. Maybe you are afraid of making mistakes or that something might happen to your baby. The list of new, previously unknown emotions is long. Because it is not just a task that you have to get through. It means a big responsibility, a decision you made out of love and the outcome of which is often unpredictable. The fact is that you have become a mother or father and you will remain one to the end of your life.

Try to take time, lots of time, it is time well spent! And try to be there for your children with patience, goodwill and compassion. That means putting your own interests on the back burner to begin with. It's not easy, but it can be done. Children can sense very well whether you are consciously available or just physically present – whether you are on your mobile phone and thinking about the next appointment, or whether you are 100 % focused right there in front of them. The more present you are, the less is the need for the little ones, and later the big ones, to vie for attention. If you do give them your undivided attention, they fill up their inner reserves of trust, security and self-confidence, and can then get by with less. They will sense relatively quickly that mummy and daddy are there when they are needed – and that they are there one hundred percent. In this way, your children build up a healthy trust in you and their close environment, in the caregivers, and develop a healthy self-confidence. This in turn benefits you as a mother or father. The first phase with a child can be dominated, then, by intensive parent-child time, but relaxing 'me time' has a place as well. This is better than persistent complaints, bad conscience and frustration on both sides, and gives you the basis for making the transition to a new phase of life successfully.

So what is the essence of being a parent? The joint desire to start a family on an emotionally and financially stable basis. The will and the willingness to put one's own ego for a while on the back burner. And, when the time comes, unconditional love for the little person and a lot of patience, serenity and even more time (see the chapter below on 'Time, perhaps the most important gift of all').

Of course there will be moments or even longer phases when being a parent seems anything but easy – when you can't live up to your expectations and everything feels like it's going against you. Then just be grateful that your wish to become the mother or father of a hopefully healthy child has come true. That is not something that can be taken for granted.

IT ALL COMES BACK TO YOU

In whatever form and whether you like it or not, children give you a whole lot back – in fact, everything you have given them. Some reactions or modes of behaviour may annoy you, others will please you all the more and you will be inclined to see them as the result of 'your parenting'. Ultimately, all reactions to a situation or life circumstance are a reflection of your behaviour and/or the result of what the children have picked up from you and your partner as caregivers and educators.

I remember one of those days during the pandemic. It was one online meeting after another, I was in my home office, both children were also at home. Home office and home studies, that usually went quite smoothly. But on this particular day I was completely stressed. I wanted to get too much done, for myself and for others, and suddenly one mishap followed another. The children, of course, sensed my negative energies and each reacted in their own way, which triggered heated discussions and in turn had an effect on me and the shape I was in that day.

Had I not become so emotional, had I explained myself briefly and apologised for my reactions, our day would have been completely different. But I couldn't do that at the time. I was distracted, angry at myself and everyone, and so I got what I sent out, in the form of stressed and irritated people who couldn't understand my mood and let themselves be dragged along or dragged down by me.

But it could also be just the opposite. Since we were all in home office, and school and studies could only take place online, it took a lot to get used to the new situation. This demanded a good deal from all of us: mutual consideration, a lot of free space and even more tolerance, primarily from me. The dining table was the office and the kitchen felt like it was in use all day. But then there were also the many nice moments when we laughed a lot and looked forward to the Netflix and Pizza evening together. And then there were the moments when, with my positive attitude as a mum, I was able to turn a bad mood into a good one.

You experience situations like this with your children every day, if not every hour, no matter what age they are. A baby knows exactly when mum is stressed or mentally absent, and reacts accordingly. Babies get restless and start crying, while toddlers try to attract attention by any means possible. Teenagers or grown ups either confront you or bat your own bad mood back at you in their own way. This doesn't make the situation any easier – isn't it just in situations like this that you are going to be most provoked by your children? In such moments you should try to stay inwardly present with yourself, and mentally step out of the energy field. This enables you to collect yourself and analyse the situation and yourself objectively, without excessive emotion.

And then suddenly the time comes when they give you 'real' presents. Suddenly you get a birthday present that is really from them, not one bought by the other parent and handed over by the children. They help in the household, go shopping or start doing things in the kitchen. Long story short, they get involved in everyday family life. And not because you have bribed or begged them beforehand, but simply because they have noticed what needs to be done. Of course, not all the home chores are taken off my shoulders. But there are moments when I am very proud of them because I see them doing things and taking responsibility. Situations that show me that what I have tried to live out for them is bearing fruit, and that they will take something of it with them into their future lives.

Looking back, I now know that one's mood usually reflects back on one immediately, but sometimes it only happens years later. How you live and what you exemplified, how you gave yourself ... How often were you dishonest, stressed and absent-minded? Or were you patient, loving and simply 'there' for your children?

SETTING AN EXAMPLE AND LETTING EXPERIENCE HAPPEN

Setting an example – an absolutely central topic for me, which is very much related to the topic of honesty (see the chapter on 'Honesty'). This applies in general as well as to life as a parent. You set an example of how you feel, think, what you laugh about and what makes you sad – and also how you deal with different challenges and people. Are you problem-focused or solution-oriented? Can you admit mistakes or is it always someone else's fault? You can talk as much as you want, but your children will only believe you if your actions match your words.

Every mother and father would like to model their best self to their own children, but sadly this doesn't always succeed. Parents are not perfect. And that's why you inevitably set a less than optimal example for your children. Often you only succeed in realising this, and then being able to stand by it, when you are called out subsequently or when the result of your actions is literally 'in front of you'. Because no parent consciously sets a negative example, after all.

As already mentioned, setting an example means that you live something. By doing things the way you think they should be done, you get results. Your children take their cue from you. The smaller they are, the greater the effect of your actions. You are the closest person they relate to. Your children sense your moods and react to them. They see your behaviour and your facial expressions, and they copy you. They observe and learn how you react to situations or people – when you are happy, sad or afraid. The older the children get, the more influences they receive from outside. Through school, friends and extra-familial activities, children begin to compare and contrast their view of life with the opinions and lives of others. They question many things and often rebel against them. Because hardly any teenagers find their parents consistently cool at this age. Especially not when binding agreements have to be made. On the one hand, the parents' ideas rarely coincide with the young people's ideas; on the other hand, boys will try to test the limits. They should be allowed to have their experiences, yet parents naturally have reservations or are even afraid. After all, they are a few years richer in terms of life experience.

I don't know about you, but there comes a time when someone who only talks and never acts is no longer believed. Someone who acts without talking is often difficult to understand. However, if you realise and feel as a child that your parents think, talk and act in the same way, then you will learn a lot of important things for your healthy development. You can't pretend to your children indefinitely, you can't set an example when it isn't you. It is a tightrope walk between 'wanting' and 'being able to'. Living this consistently as a parent and adult person, if your actions do not match your personality, will eventually cause you to break down. Ultimately, this discrepancy also reflects a dishonesty towards you and your children. And it is precisely this feeling, this experience, that the children will take with them into their personal development, and possibly later as a pattern into their own parenthood.

I will come clean here. For a very long time, far too long, I convinced myself that I could pretend anything with my children. I was sure of that. It was actually a trivial thing, the cigarette smoked in secret on the terrace. At first, my children would just say, 'Mummy, you smell so weird.' Eventually they caught me in the act. By then, at the latest, I could save my excuses. These are little things, but they are incidents that children remember well into adulthood. And they can judge you harshly for it.

My parents also smoked, even in the car. It seemed they weren't bothered if we almost got sick in the back seat.

My point is that in both situations the parents are failing to be good role models. My parents stood by their vice, they didn't hide it, whereas I actually believed for many years that I could fool my children about it. The worst thing is that the children don't come to you and say, 'Mummy, it's okay, we know you smoke.' Instead, they leave you in your delusion, make up their own minds and the subject is never alluded to.

The example of smoking is a walk in the park compared to other things we model for our children, firmly believing they will not realise what is really going on.

Moods that are present in the room can have a much more traumatic effect on children. When parents argue, it is usually audible. But if problems remain unspoken, while the father is often bad-tempered and the mother is sad, this puts an enormous strain on the children. With their fine antennae, they sense immediately when something is wrong. They are sad, worried and when the mother tries to comfort them with 'No, no, everything's fine!', it makes them totally hesitant to trust their own intuition. They doubt their gut feeling, or think that being sad and angry has to be laughed away or suppressed – that you mustn't let negative feelings come to the surface if you can help it.

I often told my children, primarily my son who was more likely to ask, that 'Everything was fine' – even though I was far from being in a good mood, was unhappy at times and didn't want to get out of bed in the morning. It takes a lot of effort to act as if all is well with the world, to laugh, play and talk as if you are in the best of spirits. Of course, I wouldn't explain to a toddler the worries that plague me in my relationship, for example. Finding an age-appropriate way to communicate is enormously difficult. But you can always take away some of a child's insecurities with clear and simple words. And at some point, when the children get older, you can answer their questions honestly. This is necessary at the latest when your children reach an age where they want to enter into relationships themselves. Then they are old enough for topics no longer to be taboo. A situation or even a partnership is neither good nor bad. But it triggers good or less good feelings in you. Try to explain why something triggers a feeling in you. But also try to explain honestly and clearly why you don't want to talk about something at the moment. They can accept this as soon as they realise that you take them seriously and are being honest. Also try to name feelings – always respectfully, never judgmentally. In this way, a child also learns to name a 'vaguely weird gut feeling' as such, and does not experience it as something that has to be ignored, suppressed or numbed. As a result, everyone learns what may be going on in them and in others and why.

I don't believe that children always seek the reason for home or family disagreements and difficulties in themselves – unless, perhaps, the parents are arguing about educational issues or the lack of free time. Of course younger children are more likely to be fobbed off with a dishonest answer. But this rift can be repaired when the mood at home improves, and you can explain to the children at a later time why you were sad or angry. And if you as a mother or father really mean your 'everything is fine' after you have had a fight, the children will be able to get the measure of their uneasy gut feelings and recover stability.

I am convinced that children recognise a congruence between thinking, talking and acting very early on. My son 'knew', even before we announced our separation, that this was going to happen. I felt very guilty about it. He also told me that it is not good to receive a clearly wrong answer, although even as a child you already feel that something is wrong. I imagined him falling asleep with that uncertain feeling in his stomach. Terrible. But because we talked about a lot of things during and after the separation, we were able to answer his questions from back then and repair the damage. When your grown-up child tells you, 'Yes, now I understand what was going on with you guys,' you can trust that.

You may be asking yourself, what do such events have to do with setting an example? Well, in every family, in all relationships, there are discussions, quarrels or temporarily difficult situations. Pushing them away or laughing them off does no one any good at all. Finding a solution, instead of sinking into the problem and letting it get bigger and bigger, is the important thing. Our children will frequently be faced with difficult situations. If they have learned from us parents to ignore problems and keep quiet, they will never be able to solve them in the long run. There are no problems without a solution, even if it is rarely easy. You just have to be willing and brave enough to go the distance. And that is exactly what we have to teach our children, by setting them an example.

Every child in a family experiences situations differently; depending on age, character and personal environment, the focus is directed differently and individual pieces of the puzzle, even supposedly unimportant statements or actions, are perceived in a different way. For example, I believe that our daughter experienced the separation completely differently, although we lived it out for both of them it in exactly the same way. During her childhood, she copied certain behavioural patterns from me or her father. Influenced by her character, her different position in the family and her environment, she perceived and lived through this whole process in her own personal way. We have no influence on the way in which our children perceive things. We can, however, ensure, with clear and honest statements and answers, that every child, every person close to us, has the opportunity to form their own opinion. Clear communication can only take place if we are honest with the children and accordingly with ourselves.

If you as a mother or father are aware of what example you are setting for your children, it also gives them space to be able to experience something. How does it feel when my parents argue at top volume, and then find a solution? Or how does it feel when both keep silent for days? How does it feel when people talk to each other respectfully and listen to each other? As a child, I did not experience the best culture of conflict in my family; when something was brewing, silence was the order of the day.

And I took this type of communication with me into my first relationship. There, however, I was able to witness discussions at the family table that seemed very loud and violent to me to begin with. But when I realised that no one was hurt or angry afterwards, I realised that this was certainly the better way to deal with a problem.

A SMALL
MENTAL LEAP ...

I mentioned that when my son told me 'OK, now I understand you', I believed him. Likewise, I was grateful when my daughter, in her always very direct way, gave me her opinion on something I said or did. I myself set a different kind of example for them, but I was able to learn a lot from them later on. I was unclear in my statements, didn't have the courage to speak my mind openly and honestly. Not out of malice, more out of fear of upsetting someone or having to explain myself. I often said 'Yes' when I meant 'No'. So I have also been inclined to cast doubt on other people's answers. Does this person really mean it or does he/she just want to protect me or avoid disappointing me?

But the solution is quite simple: if you listen to yourself, if you are honest with yourself, then you can make clear statements or announcements that do never ask for justification. You are simply authentic and honest, and that's what you radiate. No one will think to ask further.

Babies come into this world pure and unscripted, crying or screaming when they are uncomfortable and laughing when they are happy. Toddlers talk without a second thought when they have something to share. They haven't yet started to observe the rules of society. But at some point, every person begins to conform to certain norms. And then it is necessary not to lose yourself. In the midst of norms and conformity, you must never forget what you personally want to achieve and who you want to be.

So, to conclude, allow yourself and your children to be honest and to express their feelings and needs freely – always respectfully, for their good and thus for the good of all.

HONESTY

Honesty is a great concept. It is being true to your word, to yourself and to others. Honesty means being sincere and not making omissions. And it requires being able to admit mistakes. Think about how many times a day you are dishonest, with others and with yourself. I don't mean deliberately and maliciously lying to someone, but simply being less than truthful out of false concern for people's feelings or fear of consequences. One says that little lies make everyday life easier and avoid arguments! Well, that may be true, but it should not be an option in everyday family life with children.

How often does your partner, your son or your daughter ask you if everything is OK? How often do you answer with 'Yes, everything's fine'? – when at the same time you are gritting your teeth or holding back the tears? How often do you say 'Yes' to something you would rather have answered 'No' to? This may sound so trivial and unimportant now, but it can form a habit and a pattern, and eventually you find yourself answering most of the time diametrically differently from the way you feel.

Dishonest statements can deposit mental rubbish in you or even build up into a huge structure of lies. Mental rubbish may sound rather dramatic, but think about what you set off in your head: from a guilty conscience to anger at yourself – because you didn't dare to be honest yet again – to the stress of who you can tell what, and who is not allowed to know. An unnecessary mental carousel that only robs you of energy.

Very many people claim to be honest. And they believe it. Because it is not done consciously or maliciously. You expect honesty from your partner, from your children, actually from anyone who means something to you. And children expect honesty from their parents. Because how else are they supposed to learn that this is one of the most important human skills? Most of the time, people are not completely honest under the pretext that they don't want to upset or even hurt the other person. The truth often hurts a lot. But it is even more painful to uncover a tissue of lies after many years have passed.

Honesty is a big concept, a huge topic. Since this book is about children, the question arises: What should and must children know at what age? What plays out on the couple level, and what on the parent level? And what should be discussed with the children, what questions should be answered honestly? And when should a parent explain that a certain topic is better suited for a later time when they are older?

I don't think it's good to discuss relationship problems with children that affect you as a partner or the two of you as parents. That's what friends or a therapist are for. But the children, with their extremely sensitive antennae, have a right to know where they stand. They sense tension in the air: they take it to bed with them, and go to school with it in the morning. And they are completely unsettled. It is our responsibility to explain the situation to them in an age-appropriate way. It is not good if they lose trust in their gut feeling just because the parents are dishonest. Children still feel that something is wrong, but believe in the 'positive' answer they have been given. So the parental statement no longer agrees with their intuition. This must not be allowed to happen.

When it comes to honesty, one should first start with oneself. Once you realise how much easier it is to live with a congruence of feeling, thinking, speaking and acting, you will be very careful to pass this on to your children.

LOVE AND SELF-LOVE

Unconditional love is what children need in order to develop healthily. Can we really give them that?

With love, a great many hurdles can be overcome. In the context of children, I understand hurdles to be those recurrent phases where 'It all gets to be too much'. Too little sleep, stress at work, possibly sick children at home – one unfortunate circumstance follows the next. But with deep, and above all unconditional love you 'survive' these phases. When I say unconditional, I mean 'not tied to anything'. You don't love your children only if they are nice and well-adjusted – or, at a later stage, only if they bring home good grades, don't cause trouble and become successful in their job. Even without all that, no matter which way they go, you are there for them, you love them.

Children notice whether they are loved unconditionally, or only receive special attention when they have done something great. This must not be allowed to happen.

What is the precondition for this love? Self-love, being able to love and appreciate oneself. This has nothing at all to do with egoism, still less with narcissism. No, it is the basis for a healthy and strong self. A self that does not have to be constantly vying for the attention of others, that does not constantly put itself in the centre of attention and expect applause for outstanding achievements. A self that goes through the day calmly, and does things for the benefit of others, not to make itself more desirable. Love is also reassuring because it gives security. And so does self-love. It gives you security and takes away the stress of always frantically looking for recognition.

I know from personal experience that self-love can be learned later. Few people relate to themselves and their bodies in a loving and appreciative way. They criticise themselves too much, feel they are not beautiful, not smart, not successful. They do many things for others and completely forget to take care of themselves. This does not feel good, the heart and the body cry out for attention and appreciation.

And that is why every mother – and every father – must make sure they are doing well in all areas. Physically, psychologically, privately, at work and financially. It doesn't matter what order you put them in, but each of these areas should be at the highest possible level. And that means work: making sure every day that you do something good for your body and your mind, and taking care to the people you surround yourself with. If possible, only those who are good for you and don't drain your energy. Your work outside from home should also be fun, a break from parenthood. You should be grateful for everything you have achieved, not always wanting more. And most importantly, you should have confidence in yourself. For every problem and every difficult situation there is a solution. But concentrate on the solution, rather than drowning in problems, worries and fears.

All this calls for work and discipline. If you don't have this discipline to begin with, make a plan for your 'me time'. For example, resolve to have a beautiful, stress-free start to your day. Maybe with a coffee or tea on the balcony or in the garden, a refreshing shower or a sports session outside in the fresh air. Whatever suits you best. Plan it in the evening, set your alarm clock and get up earlier than your children, so that you can enjoy your time without any pressure – even if you might still be a little tired. I am convinced; you will quickly notice how well this hour or half-hour in the morning kick-starts your positive day.

This plan also helps you actually to get up, and not stay in bed until the screaming from the children's room wakes you up. My experience was that if I went for a walk in the morning, or did sport before the whole family was awake, it didn't matter what happened after that. I could handle my day with ease – not always, but most of the time.

You also need a plan so that you can redesign your daily routine. If you can stick to your project for a few weeks without giving in to convenience, then your new start in a day will soon be as much a part of your routine like brushing your teeth every night.

This 'me time', this attention that you give yourself personally, opens your heart and makes you really contented and happy – because you are finally taking the time to look after yourself. This is how self-love develops and how you can love unconditionally. You get away from the constant desire to be admired, to receive applause. I have nothing at all against admiration and recognition. Every person needs that to a healthy degree, and certainly deserves it. But be careful: are you doing something just to impress others – for applause and admiration – or is it really about something that makes you happy? Your children will copy your behaviour, they will behave in the same way to get recognition. They are afraid of coming home with bad marks, they get the feeling early on that they must fit into a pattern in order to be good enough, smart enough or beautiful enough. And that has a very unhealthy effect on development. But, as I said, you can still learn self-love in adulthood.

I once told a friend that I always look forward to getting up in the morning. And this is still the case today. Of course, even for me there were and are days where I don't start out so full of energy. But lying in bed and looking forward to an eventful day, to be able to take time for yourself and then enjoy that day, that is pure luxury. And by enjoy I mean to live everyday life – whether household stuff, office work, appointments, whatever – without stressing yourself out and with conscious gratitude. And imagine how much good you do for your family in the morning when you start the day in a good mood. There is this saying: 'Happy wife, happy life'. Although this statement doesn't quite fit the situation I am describing here, I think there is still a connection. I often felt like the 'mood setter' in the family. When I am OK, when I am in balance and at peace with myself, then the people around me are also OK. That's why I think it's necessary for us in the family to make sure that we often have positive thoughts, which in turn boosts our mood significantly. And this way we can transfer them to others.

When you have children, life can no longer be planned. By that I mean you can't make rigid plans, without allowing for deviations. You have to keep a certain flexibility, or get used to adapting. But you can also allow yourself to maintain or find your own rhythm. Set yourself daily or weekly goals and thus bring structure and more peace into your turbulent life. As a mother and housewife who may still be working – and I am referring here to the main caregivers of the children – you have a lot to juggle. With a bit of structure, you are guaranteed to be happier in the evening, even if only part of your workload is accomplished, than if you spend the whole day haphazardly, constantly distracted by something, lost in your thoughts and running against the clock. If you also make a point of getting up a little earlier in the morning to take time for yourself, you can do that too. Maybe not seven days a week, but often enough to recharge your batteries again and again.

If you really manage to teach self-love and love, you will give your children a whole bundle of life skills for their healthy development.

TIME, PERHAPS THE MOST IMPORTANT GIFT OF ALL

Objectively viewed, all people, young and old, from infants to the elderly, they all have the same number of hours per day at their disposal. But the subjective perception of time could not be more different. Depending on age, depending on the situation and depending on how you feel at the moment.

Based on their development, young children don't yet have the ability to picture time to themselves. Until the age of 2, they live almost exclusively in the present. They have no concept as yet of yesterday, later on or tomorrow. That's why it's important always to link time with a concrete example: When this is done, then we will go. One more sleep, then we travel. It is usually from the age of five that the linguistic and cognitive differentiation between tomorrow, yesterday or a week ago begins. But here, too, it makes sense to work with examples. The more the children are shown with concrete examples, the sooner they can imagine events in the future (and the past). We adults often move far too fast; we go through the day in a rush because our 24 hours are packed, we think faster and are quicker on our feet than children, simply because of our physical size. If we impose our speed, we are not being a good role model. On the contrary – we cause frustration and, at best, the children will try to stop us in our tracks.

It is therefore not surprising that our perception and idea of time is so extremely different from that of our children. As a rule, our everyday life is 'clocked' or, to put it more positively, structured. Sometimes better, sometimes worse. Especially when parents work and the children go to day care, a certain schedule is unavoidable.

And it is up to us parents to organise this in such a way that neither we nor the children have to race against time every day so we are under constant stress. Because, as already mentioned, the more we adapt to the children's pace, the faster we reach our goal. I'm not saying we have to fall completely in line with the children's steps. Sounds illogical? But that's how it is! Sure, I can't wait 30 minutes for my toddler to finish building his Lego train, or for my daughter to decide which dress she wants to wear to nursery. But still, children can't as yet think and walk in step with their parents. And so it's up to us to make certain adjustments. Believe me, it's worth it!

I've already mentioned my example with the nursery in the morning. Get everything ready for the day, get up early enough, allow enough time so that ten minutes more or less do not matter. The fact that you don't run out of the house stressed is one positive point. But above all, you radiate serenity and calmness, and this is reflected in your children. And so, even if a schedule has to be adhered to, nothing stands in the way of a good start to the day.

Every child starts to walk, talk and get beyond nappies when he or she wants to, and not when it seems appropriate to us parents. But I also know that you will get many funny looks and questions if your daughter only starts walking at 18 months. Or your own mother says, 'You're still buying nappies? Well, you were not wearing diapers anymore with12 months ...' Such remarks, which are quite unnecessary, should not and must not make you doubt your parenting. Because today my daughter is a healthy and independent young woman, just like her day-care peers who were already walking at 8 months.

We adults often run from one deadline to the next. A job, a household, a spouse, parenting, hobbies and a social life – it's not easy to balance all of these in a satisfying way. That's why I advise you, even if you don't like to hear it, to put your needs on the back burner. Prioritise and remember that less is more. Enjoy a relaxed afternoon with your little ones, without being preoccupied by thoughts of what to wear this evening. Without being on WhatsApp with your girlfriend or on the phone with your work colleague. Be in the moment, consciously and without distractions. Because it is precisely this mental absence that your children notice. Mummy (or Daddy) is physically present, but always somewhere else in her or his mind. Sentences like 'Hurry up', 'Wait a second' or 'I'll be right there', over and over again, make children sad and frustrated. Be consciously present, because then your child will suddenly let go of you of its own accord. If you are not, you will miss out on many beautiful moments that will never come back.

Your child doesn't want to 'crash' your quiet evening on purpose. Your child is not having a screaming fit at the supermarket cash desk just in order to show you up. It is simply overwhelmed by a feeling, by various impressions and incidents, and it draws attention to itself. Sure, nobody wants a screaming child at the supermarket checkout, but there is always a story behind it. It doesn't feel understood and it can't, as yet, express itself clearly. Mentally, you are already past the checkout, in the car, on your way home and cooking. But if you take the time, the child's time, to find out what made your child cry, then together you will find a solution because you will build a connection with the child and it will feel taken seriously. But you need time for that, and young mothers – myself back then included – don't have much time. They are often stressed, already thinking about their next appointment. So it's hardly surprising if the children prefer to go shopping with their dad at the week-end, rather than with their stressed-out mum during the week. Yes, children are very time-consuming, but nobody believes that beforehand. Every parent has to experience this for themselves. I don't present myself as a supermom, on the contrary. But from the moment I started getting up extra early in the morning to have time for my daughter's rhythm, before we left for the daycare or went for a walk, from then on those mornings were really relaxed.

And from my personal experience as the daughter of a mother who is now 95 years old, I know that here too slower is often faster. The more she tries to adapt to my rhythm, the more difficult, and ultimately slower everything is for her. If I think or talk too fast, even at my pace, which is no longer super-fast, she can't keep up. So, I have to repeat myself. And at the end of the day, that takes up just as much time as if I had slowed down my pace from the start. Is that why they say old people become children again?

This time during which you have to put your needs and your ego on hold is extremely short. It goes very quickly and you then reach a point where the children no longer want your presence all the time. And that is why it is worth it. Every minute that you invest in your children, honestly and lovingly, is time invested in the best possible way.

BEING CONSISTENT, OR BATTLING FOR VICTORY AND DEFEAT

In matters of upbringing, being consistent is very often seen as an absolute. Today I view this very critically. Probably because I couldn't always be consistent, or perhaps I didn't want to be? It is very difficult, but I have done all right in this area. A little side note; you have to be able to put up with inconsistency. How often did I get uncomprehending reactions when I didn't 'follow through' with something in the eyes of others? If you are not consistent, they say, there will be consequences. Many people are of the opinion that otherwise the children will just play tricks on you. For me, this principled attitude is perhaps a bit too dogmatic.

As a parent, you can't always be consistent in every possible situation. Your children have different characters, so different situations arise from different emotional states. Parenting should not be something rigid, something that follows a textbook. You have to be able to respond to your children, to each one individually. But that doesn't mean, of course, that you should move like a flag in the wind – no way!

For me, examples of these 'consistency issues' are, for instance, eating and sleeping habits, pocket money and punishments. Often these very points led to heated discussions among mothers (and fathers) and occasionally increased my insecurity in the past.

I still remember well what it used to be like when my son came home from kindergarten. It wasn't lunch time quite yet, and in consistency, you don't snack between meals. At least that's how I was brought up. But he was always so hungry – and tired, a difficult combination – and I couldn't possibly make him wait until his big sister was home from school too. So, I offered him a little something. His blood sugar went up, so did his mood, and to this day it hasn't affected his eating habits. If I had stuck to principle, we would have clashed loudly always before lunch; lunch break and relaxation would have sunk without trace. For me, it would have been a battle against a small boy with a

46

big appetite, which I could certainly have won, but without responding to his needs – or to my nerves.

This also includes evenings where you really only long for rest – or for the children to be asleep – but there is still a lengthy bedtime ritual on the agenda. You lie restlessly on the bed, silently begging your son to drop off, because the glass of wine is waiting or you desperately want to talk to your girlfriend on the phone. Finally, you sneak out quietly, and as soon as you leave the room there is a wide awake and very demanding cry of "Mamaaaaaa!?!?!" These were moments when I froze and which irritated me terribly. I stomped back – and I say this today without a guilty conscience – and I lay down on the bed again. My son was well aware of my impatience, and set out to try it to the uttermost. I actually imagined that I could make him fall asleep by breathing in and out calmly, but no way. It was all about my own inner restlessness, and as long I could not become calm, my little boy was not going to fall asleep. Today, I am convinced, and know from my own experience, that the time I took back then was time well spent. Because whether you lie still and in peace for the small person next to you, or whether you wander back and forth – getting progressively irritated, mainly because of your own restlessness – it always takes exactly the same time. So, get it right from the start. The children don't deliberately set out to deprive you of your quiet evening. Maybe they are afraid of the dark, need another goodnight story, need your voice and your closeness. But they certainly don't need a 'mum on the go' – rather a mum who lovingly, patiently and exclusively, takes time for her child. And every time I have gone with the flow, instead of trying to push through my preconceived schedule, I have been grateful for my patience, my time, my child's peacefully falling asleep, and my own clear conscience. Because there suddenly comes a time – a time determined by the children themselves – when they feel old enough to go to sleep on their own and that is what they want to do.

Here's a personal example in this regard:

'My daughter started going out at weekends at a relatively early age – in our neighbourhood, or further away towards town. Having to be home at 11 pm was too early for her. We had these discussions recurrently. I was able to go with her suggestion of coming home later, but with all her friends. They got home invariably at the appointed time and hung out as a group. I certainly didn't manage to be consistent on this point, but it wasn't a defeat for me either, just an acceptable counter-proposal on her part.'

There is no blueprint for raising children – either on the issue of going out, or on that of pocket money.

The subject of pocket money, or the first apprentice pay packet, was always (perhaps it still is?) a heated topic of discussion among parents. I remember how a colleague was quite shocked that our daughter didn't have to hand over any of her apprenticeship wages at home. No doubt about it, she was completely spoilt and would never learn how to handle money ...

Of course such statements too made me feel insecure at the time, although I was almost sure I was doing the right thing. Neither I nor my ex-husband saw why we should demand part of our daughter's wages on principle. First of all, I wanted to see how she could manage her own money for the first time. I wanted to see what she would spend it on, whether she would put something aside and whether she would be willing to shell out something for others. Today I know that I got it exactly right. My daughter works for her money, knows how to handle it and is also very generous in a loving way.

ENCOURAGE-MENT OR EXPECTATION?

As a parent, you often have the feeling that you know what is good for your children. You are older and have a lot of life experience, so this is absolutely understandable. After all, you want the best for the children and may even have an unconscious plan: either you consciously want to do it quite differently from what you yourself experienced in childhood, or you try to pass on the same identical sequence to the next generation. Nevertheless, you must never force your children into something. Don't project your missed opportunities onto your son or daughter. Be it the little boy who is dragged to football practice by his dad, or the girl who is dragooned into piano lessons. I know, these are total clichés, but even so!

I thought it was amazing when both my children wanted to learn an instrument. Wanted to? Apparently we wanted them to, because after only a few months they both stopped again. And it is still etched in their memory to this day that back then they HAD to learn an instrument! There are many similar examples – whether in the context of competitive sport, or when it comes to the choice of school and the associated further path to a university or in a vocational-practical direction. Where is the boundary between encouragement and over-expecting? Especially when parents on all sides are convinced that their child is THE high flyer? Then they push and hustle, and some things are glossed over. For a long time, I too saw my son as the next big star on the football pitch. No parents are spared this pressure from outside or the desire from within.

Today, dear parents, I know that it is sometimes damnably difficult to watch children lose motivation for the next step in their lives at what – for us parents – is just the wrong time. Suddenly school, and the upcoming entrance exams or finals, are the last things they are interested in. Trust that they will still make their way, perhaps even earn distinctions. But in terms of life as a whole, it really doesn't matter. Both my children and one of my nephews chose – again, for us parents – what was not necessarily the easiest path in their school career. But at the time, this was just what suited their pace, their will and the state of their feelings. And today? All three are successful, in both personal and professional terms.

What was important at that time was that we parents ignored our egos and the comparisons among our friends, and so could really stand behind our children. Not judging, but assessing and finding out what THEY wanted. Never mind how many parent-teacher meetings it took, or how many times the school had to be changed. Being there for them and giving support when it was needed, that was the most important thing.

As the person responsible for the child's upbringing, you often find yourself walking a fine line between encouragement and expectations – which may be excessive. Well-intentioned encouragement can quickly tip over, and the only result is that the children lose interest in learning, in school or in a hobby or give up on the home stretch.

Sometimes children, no matter what age they are, need a push or help to make a decision. Having a good talk, listening to them and finding out what they want helps enormously. And it is essential always to give them the feeling that the present uncertainty or indecision does not mean the end, there is a solution for everything. As soon as the children feel your support, some pressure is taken off, they can find a way and decide according to their own wishes and not those of the parents.

Our son, my 'up and coming football starlet', quit completely overnight after having played football for 13 years. Having told me he was thinking about taking a break, he went to his last training session that same evening. After that he gave away all his football stuff and his feet didn't touch a ball again for a long time.

COMPETITION BETWEEN SIBLINGS

I don't know any two children in the same family, with the same parents, who have been brought up in exactly the same way and have thus developed in the same direction. Every family member, children and parents alike, has a certain place within the family. This is the basis for the way they act, which in turn has an effect on the whole family structure. A dynamic that can develop positively, but also negatively. And to stop the drift into the negative or to bring it into a good direction, you have to be in the thick of it.

The more siblings there are in a family, the more personalities develop. Each one takes their place, assumes certain tasks, unconsciously of course, and all this despite the same upbringing, which just is never the same. Then you have cheerful, thoughtful, quiet, well-adjusted or very rebellious people under one roof. It is impossible to bring up every child in exactly the same way. Hopefully, there is a basic attitude in every family about what parents want to pass on to their children. And with this basis, it is important and indispensable to respond to the individual children with their respective needs. Each child feels, communicates and works through things differently. Each demands its share of time and attention from the parents. And each one wants to be loved in its own way and for its own sake, whether it is a quiet personality or more demanding.

When my children were small, I didn't feel the competition so obviously. They had few arguments with each other and the big sister took care of her three-year-old younger brother lovingly, sometimes quite firmly. She even went to bed at the same time as him, so she saved us and herself a fuss, but knew that she was allowed to stay awake a bit longer. Even then she took on a function and, perhaps unconsciously, took tension out of our family structure. She adapted, went with the flow, was quieter and demanded much less attention from us as parents. Her brother was louder, was much less able to cope with looking after himself and never let the 'umbilical cord' between him and me break. As soon as he was out of my sight, there was a demanding "Mamaaaaaa?!?" Later, when I was able to leave him alone for 30 minutes and go shopping, he called me as soon as I was out of the house: 'When are you getting back?' Of course it stressed me out, having to be present all the time. I didn't resist, though, and we built up a pattern of behaviour. But we also developed a deep trust in each other. In addition, unlike his sister, he had a time-consuming hobby, so again we paid much more attention to him than to our daughter.

This actually continued into their teenage years, almost into adulthood. When they were both grown up and could do more or less what they wanted, some stressful situations dissolved or no longer arose at all. Nevertheless, I think I can sense that our daughter is occasionally just a little bit jealous of her brother. Sharp remarks or actions towards me, not him (she loves him too genuinely for that), have confirmed the idea. I have called her on it and now we can talk openly about it. I did the same with my son. I wanted him to be aware of the situation and his place in the family.

I can no longer turn back time to redress the balance. But later on, and actually right up to the present, I tried to make up for this 'mistake' on my part towards my daughter. With a lot of understanding, goodwill and love. If, in retrospect, something has gone wrong, you always have the opportunity to explain it to your children and let them know why you acted the way you did. If you can discuss such issues with them, many obstacles are removed and the ground for deep trust and absolute honesty is created.

I also fondly remember former neighbours, friends of ours, parents of three boys and a girl. Just under 10 years younger than we were, and so were the children. I always admired them a lot, and still do. The calmness and composure with which the parents approached all their projects (and they had quite a few of those). Even the children's upbringing – perhaps the only thing that wasn't a project. I know they also had, and still have difficult situations, but nevertheless I have the impression to this day that in this family all issues that arise are approached as a challenge and not as a problem, and are dealt with to the good of all.

Some time ago, I was doing a long walk with the mother and she told me what has been going on with her family in recent years and the stresses they have been under. And there have been enough of those, believe me – from serious blows of fate and illnesses to the regular stresses of everyday family life. But the main point of this walk was for me to learn something about the competition between the siblings – three boys, each about a year apart in age, and the girl who arrived six years later.

Every child has its position in the family – be it the first born, the middle or the last. And every child makes different demands on its parents, whether because of their own personality, a weakness or even an illness. For my friend, too, the issue of time was a crucial point, where she is convinced that she did not do justice to every child. Due to an illness diagnosed in the two younger boys, the time needed for their upbringing was much greater compared to the eldest or the youngest. By contrast, the eldest had, and still has, the bonus of being the first to achieve everything – whether at school, in sports or with an exchange semester away from home. The youngest has her bonus as well: she is spoiled by her brothers, and the parents experience her first day at nursery school, children's birthdays or her last day at school consciously and knowing it to be for the last time.

The issue of time is an important one, as children can feel left behind here compared to their siblings. That is why the topic of attention should be discussed with the children from all angles, at the family table or at the bedside. Because that's where it starts. This is the only way you will notice when your children feel neglected, but only if you both are attentive. It is not always easy to sense this, especially when your children play along and adapt, like our daughter did when she was little. But it's never too late to bring this issue to the table, no matter what age. Children should realise that mum or dad notice them, even if they are not as loud, as well-read or as sporty as their brother or sister. Just this is the most effective way to bring healing.

The topic of pocket money can also become an issue among children. There are children who start a practical apprenticeship and earn their own money. Their siblings, on the other hand, study and are still dependent on the support of their parents. What is the best way to solve this? None of the children should feel financially disadvantaged because they choose a different educational path. The issue of pocket money cannot be solved in a completely fair way. Here, too, it is important, should it ever become an issue, to explain to the children that everyone has the same opportunities and can make use of them. Perhaps children in vocational training earn their own money earlier, have fewer holidays, but otherwise have more freedom and free time; while children who study full time depend on their parents and are involved in the learning process for longer, and have more holidays – but perhaps less freedom? It already starts here. It is an absolutely individual matter how each child goes about his or her education, plans leisure time and takes holidays. There is no general solution. But discussing the situation together at the family table, and looking for an answer, can certainly eliminate any difficulties and feelings of competition.

There are many such topics where children may get into competition with their siblings: sports, mobile phone use, going out ... Not every child is enthusiastic about the same sport as their siblings, and sometimes they choose no extracurricular sport or other activity at all. Another child understands the mobile phone rules made by their parents differently from their siblings. Now is this a character thing, or is there a deeper cause behind it that is directly related to the siblings? Is it compensation for something? Instead of introducing even more rules or exceptions for this one child, a discussion would certainly be more useful. Otherwise the competition, which is often not even consciously perceived by the siblings themselves, will be stoked even more. My big brother or sister can do everything, is allowed to do everything, and they confiscate my phone ...

Neither parents nor children consciously want to make life difficult for each other. Problems need to be sensitively identified. And this can only work if parents are really present, not just physically. Engaging with a child, sitting down, observing, trying to perceive moods, talking ...

There is always a reason why parents cannot care for each of their children with exactly the same intensity. It is obvious that loud, active and interested children get more attention, have more of an audience. But a quieter, more introverted and less active child needs just as much attention from the parents, and just as much of an audience and recognition, as his or her siblings.

LETTING
THEM GO

Children want a shared living arrangement with mum and/
or dad, who will keep the fridge stocked, do the laundry
and be there when you want to talk.

Depending on the educational situation, children today
often stay at home longer ... no, not longer than one would
like ... but longer than they used to.

This is also a challenge: in spite of the deliberate or desired
sense of communality, we remain parents and the children
remain children. But the children no longer want to be children in all areas, they want to enjoy the feeling of shared
living, along with the advantages of being children.

Take this as an example: three of us are living under one
roof (during the pandemic), all of us are working, the children are studying on the side. If they lived in a shared flat
(or alone), issues like laundry, shopping, waste disposal
would be absolutely not a problem – because there
would be no one else around to do these things. But here
such tasks naturally fall to the parent who is present, or so

the 'children' think. And since these same children are also experts in arguing and putting a case, there will be situations and discussions where the freedom of shared living is pitted against family rules. It's a challenge.

OK, so where do we go from here? Do I want to spoil the last months I have together with my children in the same household with arguments? Because one thing is clear to me: my part in their upbringing is complete. I can let them get on with their lives with a clear conscience. But at home they try to talk their way out of chores and evade responsibilities on a daily basis. That's why I have tried to steer a middle course between being a 'cool mum' and a constantly nagging parent. By making clear statements, I can demand certain rules for living together without spoiling the mood. Because I already know that I will miss my children incredibly. And I simply don't want these miserably prolonged, pointless discussions in our everyday life any more. Instead of starting an argument, I use the time for a brief analysis of the situation, for self-reflection and appropriate action. It all sounds terribly complicated and simple at the same time. But seriously, there is no point in starting a discussion about things that, on closer inspection, are unimportant and spoil everyone's mood.

But of course this superb feeling of serenity doesn't come every day – even though you should have experienced a lot of serenity by now through being a parent. And yes, with older children you do find you are getting older yourself ...

Again, I don't want to give the impression that I am offering my children a feel-good oasis. But I have finished bringing them up and can now 'reap what I have sown'. So have I taught them to be thoughtful and help in the household? Have they realised that the fridge and the washing machine don't fill themselves? Have they realised what it means to live together under one roof and do they appreciate it? If so, then something is coming back to me, and living together with my grown-up children will be an enrichment. But if the children selfishly treat the home as a hotel, you have to rethink and change your strategy for shared living. One day it will be time for them to move out. And then you should just let them go.

And if at times they really get on your nerves, don't take it personally. They also need to learn to disengage. Instead of criticising them, scolding them or starting an argument, close your ears for a moment, shut your mouth, find something to do and suddenly the tension is taken out of the situation. Not taking things personally is difficult, but necessary. They're annoying, you're annoying, deep down you're sad that your babies are already so big and they're just as sad that they'll soon have to leave the nest.

WHAT IF YOU CAN'T GO ON?

I don't want to waste too many words on that. Only: Get help!

There are many different reasons why your whole family life can suddenly feel like it's going down the drain. Maybe you are 'just' exhausted. I say 'just', because of course it's much more than that. This feeling of being overwhelmed, empty and totally exhausted doesn't go away by getting a little more sleep. The mornings when you don't want to get out of bed become more frequent, you can only drag yourself through the day, constantly close to tears or a meltdown. Shopping and cooking are altogether too much for you, just the thought of it makes the noise in your head even louder. It's a terrible state, I know it from my own experience.

It isn't easy to admit to yourself that you need help. And not necessarily from your best friend. See your family doctor or a therapist. These are professionals who can find out why you are feeling so miserable, and they can take away some of your fear, give you encouragement, give you ideas for getting out of this downward spiral.

The point is this: as long as you are well, the whole family is well. If you are no longer available, the whole family ship starts to sink. In the worst case scenario, your partner doesn't support you because he doesn't know how. The children can't understand mummy or daddy as they are now, they turn away or, at worst, they feel guilty about the situation. This way you don't help anyone, everything only gets worse.

It has nothing to do with failure if sometimes you almost don't know how to go on. It is part of life. You do a great deal as a mother or father, and you can be proud of it. But in order to be able to do this demanding task really well, for everyone, including yourself, you have to make sure that you stay physically and mentally healthy. Then everyone around you will also stay healthy, so once again: Get help!

AFTERWORD

So what do children really want? First and foremost, parents they can always rely on 100 %, no matter what happens or has happened. Parents who love them unconditionally. Parents who offer protection and security, especially in childhood, and who take them in their arms and comfort and encourage them when necessary. Parents who set clear rules about what is possible in life and what better avoided. Parents who are open to discussion and, above all, explain why they think these rules are good and sensible. That is what children call for. Parents – not best friends who speak the same language and go to the same clubs!

I mentioned at the beginning that becoming a mother was the best decision I ever made. Although – luckily you don't know this beforehand – it is often a thankless task. There are phases, long or short, where the children find you exhausting, uncool and above all embarrassing. It's not always easy to put up with that. But if you can do it because you are convinced you are doing the right thing, then you can give your children a lot of important things to take on their journey. For that, you also need a sufficient reserve of self-confidence and self-love so that you can live without constant confirmation of being the coolest mum. And that includes one thing above all: Look after yourself. Make sure that you are physically and mentally as fit as possible.

While writing this book, I became aware of how often parents, in an extremely challenging phase of life, also find themselves wanting to take care of their ageing or already aged parents. You are a mother or a father, and at the same time a daughter or a son.

Still, I can consider myself very lucky because of the physical and mental health of my very old parents – or today of my 95-year-old mother. Because in this context, too, it is important to let the parents decide and do things for themselves as much as possible, with everything that they are still able to do. Talking openly and honestly about problems – be it generational conflicts, or everyday difficulties that typically occur in old age. The most important attributes are love, patience and taking time.

You can see for yourself that the circle of life closes again. What children want from their parents, parents also want from their children. Maybe not necessarily as parents, but as people. Simple, but clearly not always self-evident things.

SOME THOUGHTS OF YOUNG ADULTS

In the course of writing the book, I spoke with various people about their relationship with their parents and the influence of their upbringing on their lives today. They gave me honest answers and reflected on the ways in which they have adopted similar practices for the upbringing of their own children – if they already have children – or what things they would like to do completely differently.

'I am very grateful to my parents for my childhood. Above all, my mother was a big influence on me. Thanks to her, I have a sense of basic trust. She was always there for me as a child, teenager and even today she is the first person I talk to. When I was a child, she took me in her arms and sent me lots of love. I felt very much loved right from the start.

'My dad has his heart in the right place, but our relationship was only intimate until my teenage years. He didn't learn to deal with his feelings in his childhood and couldn't show love openly. He started projecting his fears onto us children and it was stressful. I started to rebel against him, and the intimacy was gone. Today our relationship is on a better footing. His serious illness has brought us closer together again, and he has come to see what is really important in life. Men too need to deal with their feelings and should be allowed to be vulnerable.

'My mum is my role model. Despite her age, she is very, very open and up for any kind of fun. You can have a really good laugh with her. But she also deals with her dark sides, reflects on her actions and, most importantly, on her love, which is unconditional.'

'My mum gave me/us so much love, I don't have any negative thoughts.

'My father was quite the opposite, but I was only with him for the first two years of my life and rarely saw him after that. So I wouldn't say that he contributed in any way to my upbringing.

'I didn't have as much freedom as other children or young people and found this unfair at first. But today I know that she did exactly the right thing. And if I was dishonest or messed up, I got an appropriate punishment. That too is something I can understand very well today.'

'Basically, I experienced my childhood as very happy, but a few points have crossed my mind. First, I would advise parents to let their children do more. Encourage independence, even in infancy. It starts of course with little things, like putting on shoes, putting on a jacket and all that. In this way, you give your child the confirmation that he or she is independent and thus promote self-reliance and self-confidence. Although I can't remember a specific event, I know that too many things were taken "out of my hands". This had lasting effects, right up to the present.

'Another point is the way my parents dealt with conflicts. I often witnessed my parents shouting. Arguments, no matter what the topic, were often very loud instead of having a decent and constructive conversation. That's what I'm trying to do better in my own family.

'However, my parents gave me a lot of love, something incredibly important. Which is why I am convinced that the less pleasant memories have not influenced me too much. Their love was so strong and I always felt well taken care of and appreciated, so I do see my parents as the "best" parents I could have had.

I also thought it was right how they gave me (mainly in my teens) some freedom, but with clear rules. In particular, they allowed me to go out, but I had to be back home at a certain time. At first I thought it was stupid because some of my friends were allowed to stay out as long as they liked. But then I realised these rules made me feel that I was being taken care of by my family.

'Finally, I would like to say that being a parent is anything but easy. I realise that, now that I am a mum myself. I have learned all the more to appreciate all the things my parents did for me. I also know that the perfect parent does not and never will exist. All the same, it is important to develop as a parent and to deal with your own childhood, because that is the only way you can improve things in the upbringing of your own children. Today, too, it is easier to get information. Instead of reading parenting books, you can follow a cool account on Instagram about "gentle parenting" for instance.'

'Spontaneously what comes to mind is that I would like to praise my daughter more. Where she is concerned, praise works wonders. I don't want to give her the feeling that she has to be constantly comparing herself with other children her age. Unfortunately, that was a bit too much the case in my childhood.

'But what I definitely want to do, in the same way as my mother did, is to build a bond that will last long beyond the time you live at home. Even if you are no longer living under the same roof, someone is always there to help you with whatever you need.'

'We were very lucky to have had the best possible upbringing. But you only realise that when you are a parent yourself. For us, it is essential always to stand behind the children, no matter what they do. This gives them an incredibly important and powerful feeling. Today we often ask ourselves how our parents managed to do this, at times when, in the stress of everyday, we find ourselves pushed to the limit. We try to remain objective, and don't claim we know always better than the children or get into needless discussions and arguments. This sounds quite simple, but it is often a great challenge to put it into practice.'

'I think it is very important to have good communication in the way that is appropriate for the child's age. Tell them what one's previous relationship with one's parents was like, i.e. their own grandparents. In this way, children understand that parents do not react as they do out of a lack of interest, but because they have not learned otherwise.

'Feelings should also be acknowledged, not only in the children, but also in oneself. In this way, children learn to feel themselves and sense what is going on inside them. And topics should not be made taboo. If the parents do not want to talk about it, then they should explain why.

'Letting go is always an important issue: encouraging children to go their own way. Reframing fears or being mindful in communication.

'Being aware of what parents project onto children, e.g. their own desires and life goals they may have missed out on; not imposing these on the child.'

'I was often told, "Yes, we'll do that", and then nothing happened. My parents always changed plans at short notice, which taught me spontaneity on the one hand, but gave me a lack of stamina on the other.

'As a result, today, as an adult, I sometimes change my plans abruptly and so have trouble keeping promises. But I'm aware of this and I'm working on it.'